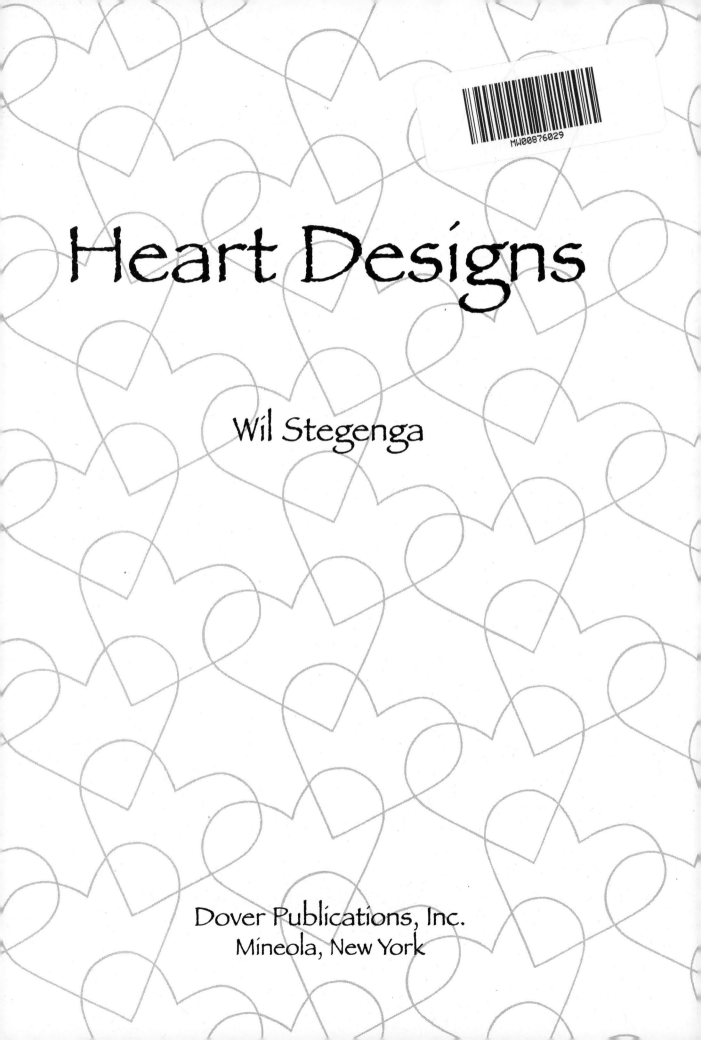

Heart Designs

Wil Stegenga

Dover Publications, Inc.
Mineola, New York

Note

Small hearts, big hearts, and stylized hearts—this coloring book has them all! The thirty designs are arranged in order by coloring difficulty, starting with easy-to-color images and ending with some challenging pieces. To color the illustrations, you can use pens, pencils, crayons, or felt-tip pens. If you combine your coloring methods you will get an interesting effect. To make them sparkle, try adding some glitter accents. When you are finished coloring, you can customize your design by adding the name of a special friend or family member onto the hearts and give the page as a gift. The book itself makes a great present for Valentine's Day, a birthday, or any day!

Copyright

Copyright © 2008 by Wil Stegenga
All rights reserved.

Bibliographical Note

Heart Designs is a new work, first published by Dover Publications, Inc., in 2008.

DOVER *Pictorial Archive* SERIES

This book belongs to the Dover Pictorial Archive Series. You may use the designs and illustrations for graphics and crafts applications, free and without special permission, provided that you include no more than four in the same publication or project. (For permission for additional use, please write to Permissions Department, Dover Publications, Inc., 31 East 2nd Street, Mineola, N.Y. 11501.)

However, republication or reproduction of any illustration by any other graphic service, whether it be in a book or in any other design resource, is strictly prohibited.

International Standard Book Number
ISBN-13: 978-0-486-46537-1
ISBN-10: 0-486-46537-3

Manufactured in the United States of America
Dover Publications, Inc., 31 East 2nd Street, Mineola, N.Y. 11501

Creative Coloring is Just a Heartbeat Away

Cascades of beautifully rendered heart designs fill 30 ready-to-color pages. Use markers, paints, crayons, or colored pencils to add vibrant hues to oceans of surging, interlocking, and spinning hearts of every shape and size! Experiment with shading techniques and creative media, and feel your pulse beat with excitement as you dream up wonderful works of art. Amazing coloring challenges that range in levels of difficulty, each illustration is fascinating and unique...just like the heart itself.

$3.95 USA   PRINTED IN THE USA

ISBN-13: 978-0-486-46537-1
ISBN-10: 0-486-46537-3

50395

9 780486 465371

UPC

8 00759 46537 8

Planet Friendly Publishing
✓ Made in the United States
✓ Printed on Recycled Paper
Learn more at www.greenedition.org

GREEN EDITION

At Dover Publications we're committed to producing books in an earth-friendly manner. To learn how this title earned the Green Edition seal, please turn to the copyright page at the start of this book.

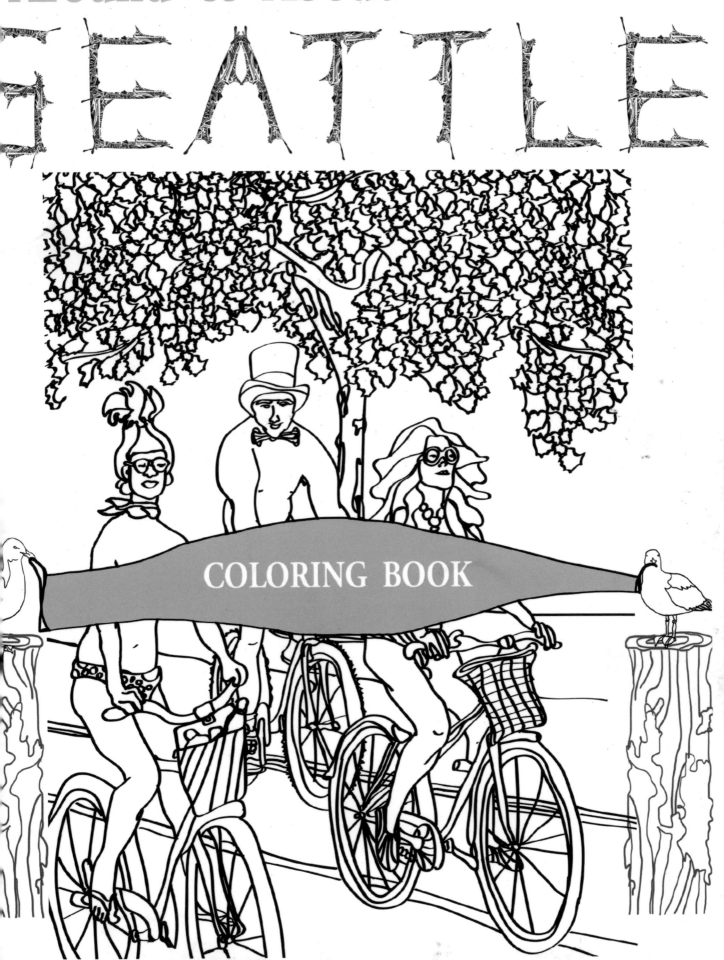